SIGHTSEERS
ESSENTIAL TRAVEL GUIDES TO THE PAST

ANCIENT
EGYPT

A GUIDE TO EGYPT IN THE TIME
OF THE PHARAOHS

SALLY TAGHOLM

KINGfISHER

KINGFISHER
Kingfisher Publications Plc
New Penderel House,
283–288 High Holborn,
London WC1V 7HZ

Editor   Julie Ferris
Senior Designers   Mike Buckley, Jane Tassie
Designer   Jill Plank

Illustrations   Inklink Firenze
Kevin Maddison

Editorial assistance   Christian Lewis, Katie Puckett
DTP Co-ordinator   Nicky Studdart
Production Controllers   Caroline Jackson, Kelly Johnson
Picture Research Manager   Jane Lambert
Proofreader   Sheila Clewley
Indexer   Sylvia Potter

First published by Kingfisher Publications Plc 1999
2 4 6 8 10 9 7 5 3 1

1TR/1298/WKT/UNV(UNV)/140MA

A CIP catalogue record for this book is available from
the British Library.

ISBN 0 7534 0321 8

Printed in
Hong Kong/China

Contents

Introducing Egypt

Visitors to Ancient Egypt will discover a country with a long and fascinating civilization that dates back thousands of years. Its history is divided into different periods – Old Kingdom, Middle Kingdom and New Kingdom. During the New Kingdom, and under the rule of Pharaoh Rameses II, it has become the greatest power in the Middle East.

Sightseers' tip Rameses II's massive construction programme is well under way and looks set to rival the golden age of pyramid building! Make sure you visit the magnificent temples at Karnak and Abu Simbel.

Rameses II came to the throne more than sixty years ago. A renowned soldier, he is famous not only for his many military campaigns, but also for having fathered over 100 children!

Writing was invented nearly 2,000 years before the reign of Rameses II. Hieroglyphs are a combination of ideograms (signs standing for ideas) and phonograms (signs standing for sound).

It was also 2,000 years ago that the tribes of Upper and Lower Egypt were united by the first pharaoh, Menes. His capital was at Memphis.

The first pyramid, the Step Pyramid, was built 1,500 years ago at Saqqara by architect Imhotep as a burial place for Pharaoh Djoser.

The great age of pyramid building lasted for about 400 years. The largest pyramid was built for Pharaoh Khufu at the pyramid complex in Giza.

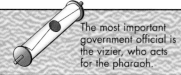
The most important government official is the vizier, who acts for the pharaoh.

The pharaoh of Egypt is believed to be the god Horus in human form.

The walls of most monuments and temples are covered in hieroglyphs.

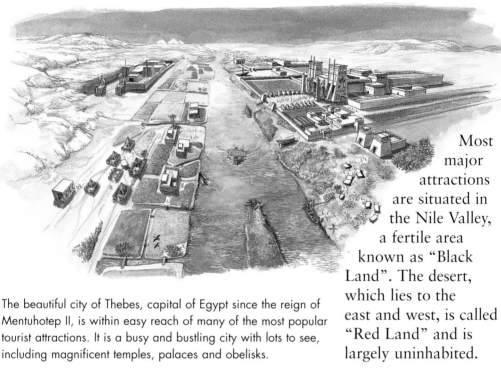

Most major attractions are situated in the Nile Valley, a fertile area known as "Black Land". The desert, which lies to the east and west, is called "Red Land" and is largely uninhabited.

The beautiful city of Thebes, capital of Egypt since the reign of Mentuhotep II, is within easy reach of many of the most popular tourist attractions. It is a busy and bustling city with lots to see, including magnificent temples, palaces and obelisks.

Five hundred years ago, Egyptian pharaohs conquered Nubia, pushing Egypt's empire 320 km south. Egyptian rule was imposed and forts, temples and towns were built. Huge quantities of gold are extracted from Nubian mines.

Tutankhamun, the "boy king", came to the throne 70 years ago, aged ten. He died nine years later and his body is believed to be buried in the Valley of the Kings, in a tomb full of spectacular treasures.

The Egyptian empire is currently at its height. Pharaoh Rameses II has fought many brave battles and ordered the construction of many monuments across Egypt.

Travelling about Egypt

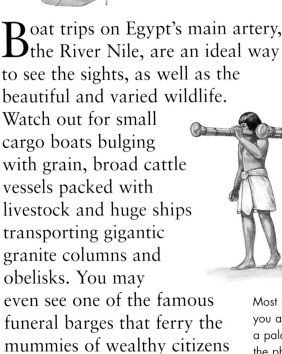

Boat trips on Egypt's main artery, the River Nile, are an ideal way to see the sights, as well as the beautiful and varied wildlife. Watch out for small cargo boats bulging with grain, broad cattle vessels packed with livestock and huge ships transporting gigantic granite columns and obelisks. You may even see one of the famous funeral barges that ferry the mummies of wealthy citizens to holy burial grounds.

Most people get around on foot in town, but if you are feeling lazy, treat yourself to a ride on a palanquin, or carrying chair, just like the pharaoh.

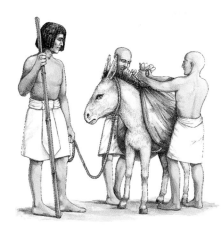

Sightseers' tip If you are planning a long expedition into the desert, it is advisable to hire a donkey. Available in most towns, they are cheap but extremely reliable.

Intrepid travellers will enjoy a day trip to the desert that lies to the east and the west of the Nile valley. The "Red Land", has a harsh and mysterious landscape that covers more than 90 percent of the entire country. Make sure that you are accompanied by an experienced guide, or join one of the many merchants' caravans travelling the trade routes to the coast.

It can get very hot in the Egyptian sun. Make sure you travel on a boat with some kind of canopy or awning to provide shade in the intense heat.

Boats are the main form of transport in Egypt and most people live close to the river. Usually made from papyrus or wood, many boats have a central sail.

What to wear

Pack the bare minimum – with daytime temperatures well over 30°C, you won't need many clothes. What you do take should be light and comfortable. A simple, white linen shift is ideal for everyday wear in town. In the country, people usually wear just a loincloth.

You will find exquisite golden jewellery made by highly skilled craftsmen. It is often inlaid with semi-precious stones from the desert, or imported stones such as turquoise.

Most people go barefoot but it is a good idea to buy a pair of plaited papyrus sandals to protect your feet from scorpions and snakes.

Sightseers' tip

Both men and women wear a thick black eye paint known as kohl. It is made from ground minerals and kept in elaborate cosmetic jars.

Pleats and fringes are the latest New Kingdom fashion with men wearing long, pleated skirts over a short underkilt, and women wearing pleated robes of the finest white linen gauze.

You will need valuable objects if you wish to barter for Egyptian jewellery.

Egyptians rub their skin with cat, crocodile and hippopotamus fat.

Magical charms are worn on necklaces to prevent sickness.

For evening wear it is important to dress in more elaborate outfits, especially if you are invited to a banquet or feast. On formal occasions both men and women wear dazzling jewellery, and braided black wigs made of human hair and held in place with beeswax. Perfumes made from oils scented with myrrh and cinnamon are popular.

Flax plants provide the linen for all Egyptian clothes – from the coarsest material to the finest gauze.

Food and drink

The wide selection of food stalls in most towns means that it is easy to get a takeaway. Bread, fruit, vegetables and beans are available to visitors on a tight budget, and delicious dried fish and wild birds are on offer to the more adventurous. Meat is very expensive and is only eaten on special occasions.

The thick, lumpy beer is made from mashed barley bread, so use a syphon!

Bread comes in all shapes and sizes. The flour is made by grinding grain between two stones.

If you are lucky enough to be invited to a banquet, you will see that wealthy Egyptians eat very well indeed. There are dozens of courses, and the menu might include duck, goose and ox, as well as delicacies such as gazelle, antelope and ostrich.

The host and important guests usually sit on low chairs or stools. Other people use mats or cushions on the floor.

Spices and herbs, like cumin, mustard and thyme are often used to flavour meals.

Watch out! Grit in the flour used to make bread might break a tooth!

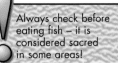
Always check before eating fish – it is considered sacred in some areas!

Don't worry about knives and forks – everyone in Egypt eats with their fingers, rinsing their hands between courses. You may notice that banquet guests often wear cones of perfumed fat on their heads. These melt during the evening, keeping them cool.

Sightseers' tip

Although beer is the national drink, why not try one of the many fine Egyptian wines? Local date or palm wines are excellent value.

11

Accommodation

A wide variety of accommodation to suit most budgets is available in all major cities. You can choose between a luxury suite in a nobleman's house, a room in an attractive town house or a cheap and cheerful stay in a poorer quarter.

Sightseers' tip Windows should be small and high to keep out the heat and dust. Houses are often built on raised platforms as many areas are badly affected by the Nile floods.

Cheap accommodation can be somewhat cramped, with several families living together. Be prepared to share a room and to sleep on the floor or on the roof.

Beds, chairs, tables and chests are usually carved out of a local wood like sycamore fig. However, cheap accommodation has little furniture.

If you are on a tight budget, why not stay out of town? Tomb-workers' village houses are simple, but excellent value. Animals are often stabled in the front room, but you can sleep on the roof.

12

Don't expect to sleep well. Egyptians use wooden headrests as pillows!

Grand houses have tiled floors and coloured ceilings and walls.

Cooking is done outside to reduce fire risk in cheap accommodation.

Top of the range rooms are available all year round in country villas owned by noble families. Cool and comfortable, they offer every amenity, including bathrooms! You will enjoy Egyptian hospitality at its best, including lavish home-made food. You can also relax in tranquil gardens by a pool brimming with fish and lotus flowers.

All Egyptian houses, from the pharaoh's spectacular palace to the humblest village home, are made of mud bricks. The mud is mixed with chopped straw, shaped into moulds and baked in the sun.

Shopping

A visit to one of Egypt's bustling markets can provide a welcome break from sightseeing. It is essential to make a day of it if you pick one of the major centres like Memphis or Thebes, and you are guaranteed to find an amazing variety of produce and goods. Mouth-watering pomegranates, melons and figs, sticky sweetmeats, olives, dates and over 30 different kinds of bread are all readily available.

Large town markets can be very hot and noisy, with traders bringing in their wares from far and wide. Shopping can take a long time – stall-holders are well trained in the art of bartering!

Egyptian craftsmen produce beautiful vases, statues and carvings in stone, wood, metal and ivory.

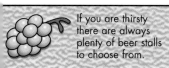
If you are thirsty there are always plenty of beer stalls to choose from.

You will find beautiful crafts for sale in palace and temple workshops.

Leave your money at home – Egyptians use a bartering system instead!

Sightseers' tip "Sniffer" baboons are a common sight in many markets. They play a vital role in the fight against crime, helping officials track down thieves.

The markets are also a very good place to shop for crafts and clothes – the kingdom has a reputation for producing the finest linen in the world! With its long history of trading with other nations, Egypt also buys a huge range of exotic goods, such as precious stones and olive oil, from neighbouring countries. If you visit one of the smaller country markets, remember that you will find only home-grown produce and locally made artefacts.

You will soon get used to the bartering system and will quickly be able to work out exactly how many fig cakes equal a gold necklace. Market officials are always on hand to sort out any disputes between traders.

Leisure time

Whether you are young or old, there is a wide range of leisure activities on offer. If possible, try to time your visit to coincide with one of the major religious festivals, which often last for several days. You can be sure of a spectacular show with acrobats, jugglers, dancers and vibrant music.

Egyptian children play with all sorts of differer toys including dolls, model animals and spinning tops. They also enjoy playing catc with balls made of clay

Egyptians love children – you will see them playing everywhere. Don't be surprised by the latest hairstyle. All boys up to 12 years of age have "side-locks".

Egypt's rich cultural heritage is reflected in the ancient art of story telling, which is handed down from generation to generation. Sit down quietly in the shade and listen to a story about the exploits of the gods, or the adventures of a crocodile in the Nile!

16

 It is said that Pharaoh Tutankhamun's tomb has four senet boards in it.

 Hathor is goddess of happiness, dance and music, as well as love.

 Some stories may be familiar – Cinderella is an Egyptian tale!

Sightseers' tip The biggest festival takes place at New Year (usually around 19th July). It marks the first glimpse of Sirius, the "Dog Star", and there is a five-day national holiday.

You can always try your hand at one of the many Egyptian board-games such as snake, which is played on a circular stone board, or senet. Leapfrog and tug-of-war are also popular games.

Music is everywhere! Musicians perform on string, wind and percussion instruments at festivals and banquets. Farmers even sing to their oxen as they thresh the corn!

Senet, one of the most popular board-games, is played with counters and small sticks. There are 30 squares which you have to cross, overcoming evils and obstacles, to reach the kingdom of Osiris.

Hunting

Unchanged since the earliest days of Egyptian civilization, the traditional hippo hunt on the River Nile makes for a thrilling excursion. Alternatively, hunting trips in the desert, once reserved for kings and courtiers, are now widely available to travellers.

Teams of hunters in papyrus boats chase huge hippos through the water. They use lassoes to catch them and spears to weaken them.

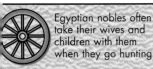
Egyptian nobles often take their wives and children with them when they go hunting.

Lion hunting is banned during the festival of the cat, when the god Bast is worshipped.

Make sure your arrows are sharp. They should be tipped with ivory, bone, flint or metal.

Sightseers' tip Hunting birds in the reed thickets of the River Nile is a popular activity. Hire of a boat is optional, but a sturdy wooden throwstick is essential.

Cats are considered sacred and often wear a golden ring. Domesticated during the Middle Kingdom, they are now used by hunters to help them catch birds and wildlife. The Egyptian word for cat is "Miw".

If you go hunting for desert hare, wild bull, gazelle, oryx, antelope or lion, make sure you are properly equipped. Bring plenty of javelins, spears and arrows, which you can store in your horse-drawn chariot. Never hunt in the desert without an experienced guide and at least one hunting dog.

19

Mummification

Egyptians believe in life after death and preserve the body by mummification. Head for the west bank of the Nile and visit one of the funerary workshops where bodies are prepared for their tombs and the journey to the next world.

As the layers of linen are wrapped round a mummy, amulets are bound in for good luck. They help to make the journey to the next world as smooth as possible.

The body is covered with natron (a compound of sodium and carbon) and left to dry for at least 40 days before being bandaged in linen.

The brain, liver, lungs and intestines are removed from the body, and dried and wrapped in linen. They are stored separately in canopic jars which are then placed in the tomb.

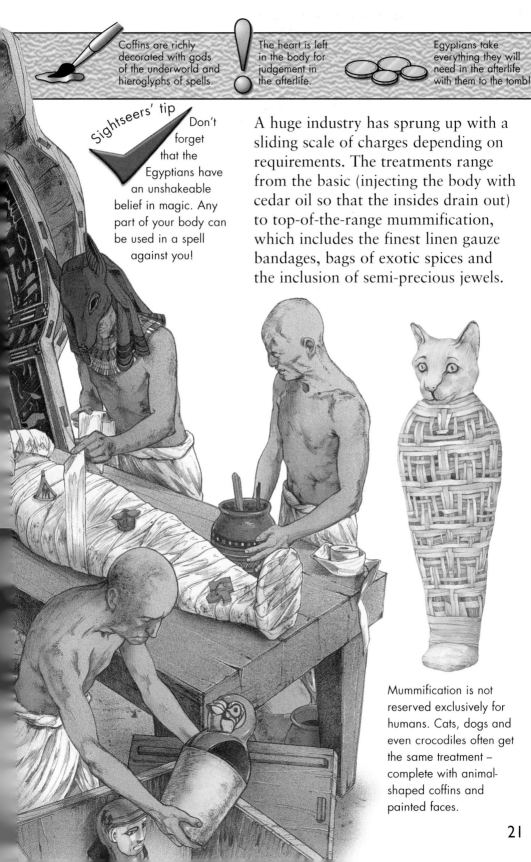

Coffins are richly decorated with gods of the underworld and hieroglyphs of spells.

The heart is left in the body for judgement in the afterlife.

Egyptians take everything they will need in the afterlife with them to the tomb!

Sightseers' tip Don't forget that the Egyptians have an unshakeable belief in magic. Any part of your body can be used in a spell against you!

A huge industry has sprung up with a sliding scale of charges depending on requirements. The treatments range from the basic (injecting the body with cedar oil so that the insides drain out) to top-of-the-range mummification, which includes the finest linen gauze bandages, bags of exotic spices and the inclusion of semi-precious jewels.

Mummification is not reserved exclusively for humans. Cats, dogs and even crocodiles often get the same treatment – complete with animal-shaped coffins and painted faces.

21

The pyramids

The three great pyramids at Giza are not only Egypt's top tourist attraction, they are also regarded as some of the greatest feats of engineering the world has ever known. They were built more than 1,200 years before the reign of Rameses II as burial tombs for pharaohs Khufu, Khafre and Menkure.

Sightseers' tip

"Tomb robber tours" are the only way to see inside the pyramids. You will be taken through huge granite doors and along a network of secret corridors and false passages.

Don't miss the famous Step Pyramid at Saqqara – the first pyramid ever built in Egypt. Designed by the great architect, Imhotep, it is the burial place of Pharaoh Djoser.

The angles of the walls of the Bent Pyramid of Pharao Sneferu at Dahshu change towards the top, giving the pyramid its distinctive shape.

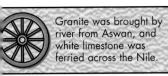

Granite was brought by river from Aswan, and white limestone was ferried across the Nile.

Many pyramids have inscriptions of magic spells to aid the journey to the afterlife.

The huge pyramid of Pharaoh Khufu took more than twenty years to build!

At 138 metres high, Khufu's pyramid is the largest stone building on Earth, and is one of the Seven Wonders of the World. It is made up of more than 2.3 million limestone blocks, each weighing at least 2.5 tonnes!

The casing of polished limestone, which gives the pyramids their smooth sides, has begun to erode.

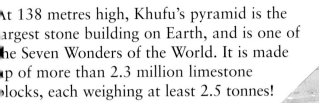

The Great Sphinx, which guards the pyramids at Giza, has a lion's body and the face of Pharaoh Khafre. Made of stone, it is 73 metres long and 20 metres high.

Farmers helped to build the pyramids during the annual floods. They used simple copper and stone tools to cut the massive blocks of stone. These were hauled up mud and brick ramps on wooden sledges.

23

Karnak

Make an early start and take a sturdy pair of sandals with you when you visit the famous Temple of Amun at Karnak, just north of Thebes. Karnak has grown over the centuries from a modest shrine to a vast temple complex. The most recent addition has only just been completed – the spectacular Hypostyle Hall has 134 gigantic pillars, each one carved and brightly decorated to look like a huge papyrus plant.

You will probably notice that the colossal statues of Rameses II currently being erected are of a scale and splendour unrivalled in previous dynasties. Finishing touches are chiselled by skilled masons.

Overlooking the Nile at Abu Simbel, an enormous temple for Rameses has been cut deep into the sandstone cliffs. It has been designed so that twice a year the rays of the Sun illuminate a statue of Rameses inside.

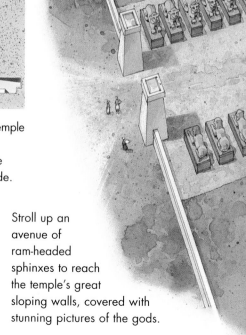

If you visit Karnak during the annual religious festival, you might catch a glimpse of the statue of Amun, king of all the gods. This is the one time it leaves its home deep inside the sanctuary to visit another temple.

Stroll up an avenue of ram-headed sphinxes to reach the temple's great sloping walls, covered with stunning pictures of the gods.

Amun is shown as a ram, a goose or a serpent, but most often as a crowned king.

The obelisks are capped with gold and covered with prayers to the gods.

You may not be allowed in the temple itself – it is usually reserved for priests.

Karnak is the most important religious centre in the whole of Egypt. It is known as Ipet-isut – "the most perfect of places". The vast complex includes workshops, living-quarters, a school, a library, a sacred pool and storehouses.

Sightseers' tip Egyptians often pray to statues of the pharaoh. This is because they believe he is descended from the gods.

An Egyptian farm

Farming is the basis of Egypt's thriving economy, with a wide variety of fruit and vegetables being cultivated on the fertile banks of the Nile. If you plan to visit a farm, make sure you avoid the inundation season (July to November), when the river floods and most of the fields are under water.

Honey is widely used as a sweetener in Egypt, and many farms have beehives.

Don't miss Egypt's famous wine-growing area in the north of the kingdom.

Travelling around is tiring. You may prefer to stay at a farm overnight!

Thanksgiving ceremonies are held at the height of the floods.

Farming methods are simple but extremely efficient. Crops include wheat and barley (to make bread and beer) and flax (to make linen).

Sightseers' tip   If you visit a farm during the ploughing or harvest seasons, you might get roped in to lend a hand!

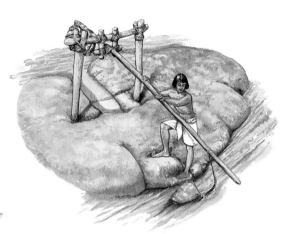

A "shaduf" is used to raise water from the Nile to fill irrigation canals. It has a bucket on one end and a weight on the other to aid lifting.

Along with mouth-watering fruits and vegetables such as melons, pomegranates, figs, onions, garlic and beans, farmers often keep cattle, sheep and pigs. Birds, including ducks and geese, are also reared for eggs and meat.

Be prepared for hard work if you go on a fishing trip on the Nile. Fishermen use small boats made of bundles of papyrus reed tied together with twine. Their fishing nets, also made of papyrus, are weighted down with stones or lead.

27

Survival guide

Plan your holiday carefully before you travel and make sure you have all essential documents. You may be refused entry to this highly bureaucratic country if your paperwork is not in order! If there is a problem, ask to see the local scribe. He will be able to draw up any document you need for a small fee.

Administration

The pharaoh is not only the king of Egypt, but also thought to be Horus, son of the sun god Re. He holds absolute civil, religious and military power. However, since the New Kingdom years have brought great military expansion, he has delegated a lot of day-to-day administration to various government departments.

You'll only see scribes writing hieroglyphs on tomb and temple walls or in important matters of state. Everyday Egyptian – a simple, joined-up version – is much easier to learn!

Law and order

Official documents always carry the seal of Rameses II to prove that they are authentic. It shows his name, surrounded by sacred symbols.

Local police keep order in most towns. However, if you are planning to venture alone into the countryside or desert, you should be wary of robbers. In Egypt, justice is carefully administered – by the vizier in the great courtrooms of the capital, and by local people in the village courts. The most common form of punishment is beating.

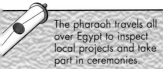
The pharaoh travels all over Egypt to inspect local projects and take part in ceremonies.

Remember – hieroglyphs can be written from left to right, right to left, or top to bottom.

If you don't win in court, you can always appeal to the local god!

Health

Egyptian doctors are highly skilled and have a detailed knowledge of anatomy. They work closely with magicians when practising medicine. Common injuries like snake bites and scorpion stings are most effectively treated with a combination of spells and medicines. Garlic is a very valuble plant, as it has both medical and magical powers.

If you want extra protection from the evil spirits that cause disease, you could invest in a magical charm, or amulet. The eye of Horus is believed to be particularly powerful.

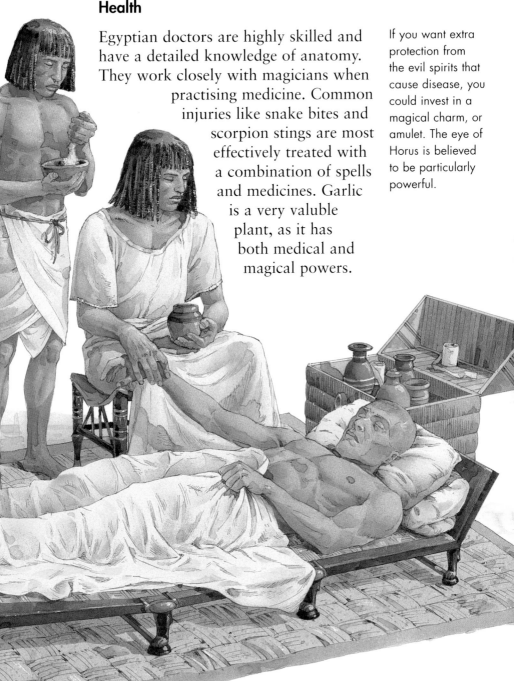

29

? Souvenir quiz

At the end of your stay in Egypt, your suitcase is probably full of exotic presents for friends at home – plus a few souvenirs for yourself! Have a go at this quiz to test your knowledge of Ancient Egypt.

1. There are many different ways to get around in Ancient Egypt. What is the pharaoh's favourite form of transport?

a) He likes to ride on a small grey donkey.

b) He travels on a large cattle vessel on the Nile.

c) He prefers to be carried about in a palanquin, or carrying chair.

2. Ordinary Egyptian furniture, such as beds and chairs, is usually carved out of which sort of wood?

a) Ebony inlaid with gold and semi-precious stones.

b) Locally grown sycamore fig.

c) Cedar wood which is imported from Lebanon or Syria.

3. Although many Egyptians go barefoot, cool and comfortable sandals are often worn. What are they made of?

a) They are made using locally grown fringed flax.

b) The sandals are made of plaited papyrus, palm fibre or leather.

c) Egyptians wear braided human hair and beeswax sandals.

4. Mummification is increasingly popular in New Kingdom Egypt – for humans as well as some cats and crocodile Where are the bodies prepared?

a) Funerary workshops on the west bank of the Nile.

b) The pyramids at Giza.

c) The oasis city of Crocodilopolis.

Some of the pyramids are lined ith hieroglyphic inscriptions. hat are they?

Directions to the pharaoh's burial amber deep inside the pyramid.

b) Official government warning to tomb robbers to stay away from the pyramid.

c) Magical spells to help the pharaoh's body rise to the skies and arrive safely in the afterlife.

You will certainly have visited me of Rameses II's spectacular w buildings, which include an citing addition to the Temple of mun at Karnak. What is it?

The Temple of Amun at Luxor.

Colossal gold-capped obelisks scribed with hieroglyphs.

The Hypostyle Hall th its stunning 134 gantic, painted lumns.

7. Although Rameses II holds absolute civil, religious and military power, he has been forced to delegate some authority. Who is second-in-command?

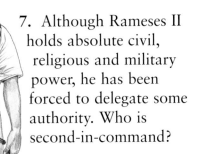

a) Horus, the son of Re, the sun god in human form.

b) The chief minister, or vizier.

c) A trained magician who has detailed knowledge of spells and the properties of plants.

8. You will probably have tried your hand at one of the many board games enjoyed by Egyptians, young and old. Which of these popular games was buried with Tutankhamun?

a) Senet – using counters and a throwstick, you have to overcome obstacles and evils to reach the kingdom of Osiris.

b) Snake – using small stone balls, you have to reach the centre of a circular board, coiled in the shape of a serpent.

c) Pythons and pyramids – an ancient version of snakes and ladders.

Index

Acknowledgements

Design assistance
Joanne Brown

Inklink Firenze illustrators
Simone Boni, Alessandro Rabatti, Lorenzo Pieri,
Luigi Critone, Lucia Mattioli, Francisco Petracchi,
Theo Caneschi.

Additional illustrations
Vanessa Card, Julian Baker, Peter Dennis, Francesca
D'Ottavi, Luigi Galante, Nicki Palin, Mark Peppe,
Richard Ward.

Picture credits
b = bottom, c = centre, l = left, r = right, t = top
p.4c The Ancient Egypt Picture Library; p.7cr

AKG/Erich Lessing; p.8c Egyptian Museum,
Cairo/AKG/Erich Lessing; p.14cl Kunsthistoriches
Museum, Vienna/AKG/Erich Lessing; p.17cr E.T.
Archive/British Museum; p.19t E.T. Archive/British
Library; p.20bl E.T. Archive/Louvre Paris; p.22bc
& b The Ancient Egypt Picture Library; p.28c
Rockefeller Museum, Jerusalem (IDAM)/AKG/Erich
Lessing; p.28bl E.T. Archive/Egyptian Museum Cairo

*Every effort has been made to trace the copyright
holders of the photographs. The publishers apologise
for any inconvenience caused.*

Souvenir quiz answers

1 = c)   2 = b)   3 = b)   4 = a)   5 = c)   6 = c)   7 = b)   8 = a)

*Rameses II reigned from
1289–1224 BC.*